U.S. ENVIRONMENTAL PROTECTION AGENCY

OFFICE OF INSPECTOR GENERAL

Costs Claimed by the North Carolina Rural Economic Development Center, Inc., Under EPA Grant No. X96418405

Report No. 12-4-0499   May 23, 2012

Report Contributors: John Trefry
                                             Phil Cleveland
                                             Bill Spinazzola

Abbreviations

CFR	Code of Federal Regulations
EPA	U.S. Environmental Protection Agency
FY	Fiscal year
NCREDC	North Carolina Rural Economic Development Center, Inc.
OIG	Office of Inspector General
OMB	Office of Management and Budget

At a Glance

Why We Did This Review

The U.S. Environmental Protection Agency (EPA) Office of Inspector General is examining assistance agreements to nonprofit organizations. We selected the North Carolina Rural Economic Development Center, Inc., (NCREDC) for review. The purpose of the review was to determine whether the NCREDC complied with grant requirements and applicable regulations.

Background

EPA Region 4 issued to the NCREDC Grant No. X96418405, in the amount of $994,100, to help fund a $1,046,421 project under Section 104(b)(3) of the Clean Water Act. The grant was amended to increase funding, bringing the total award to $1,192,500. The grantee, which also received funding from state sources, incurred costs of $2,204,031 between October 1, 2003, and May 31, 2007.

For further information, contact our Office of Congressional and Public Affairs at (202) 566-2391.

The full report is at:
www.epa.gov/oig/reports/2012/
20120523-12-4-0499.pdf

Costs Claimed by the North Carolina Rural Economic Development Center, Inc., Under EPA Grant No. X96418405

What We Found

The NCREDC did not comply with the Code of Federal Regulations (CFR), specifically 2 CFR Part 230, regarding financial management. The NCREDC did not properly allocate direct costs between state and federal funding sources. Therefore, EPA should recover $1,192,500 in costs questioned under the grant. The NCREDC failed to properly allocate the questioned costs primarily because EPA provided incorrect guidance and inadequately monitored the grant. Region 4 must recognize that the $178,556 budget revision it directed is not allocable to the EPA grant because it shifted subcontract costs allocable to state funding sources to the EPA grant. Additionally, the NCREDC was unfamiliar with federal grant regulations.

What We Recommend

We recommend that the Regional Administrator, Region 4, disallow all costs paid under Grant No. X96418405 and recover $1,192,500.

Planned Agency Corrective Actions

Region 4 and the NCREDC disagreed with our draft findings and recommendation. We evaluated the information in their responses to our draft report but did not modify our findings or recommendation. The recommendation is thus unresolved with resolution efforts in progress.

Region 4 provided a corrective action plan indicating that the NCREDC will submit a plan outlining full accounting of the allocation of costs between state and federal funding sources for the project. With the NCREDC's plan, the region can determine the reasonableness, allocability, and allowability of costs in accordance with the provisions of the applicable federal cost principles.

UNITED STATES ENVIRONMENTAL PROTECTION AGENCY
WASHINGTON, D.C. 20460

May 23, 2012

MEMORANDUM

SUBJECT: Costs Claimed by the North Carolina Rural Economic
Development Center, Inc., Under EPA Grant No. X96418405
Report No. 12-4-0499

FROM: Arthur A. Elkins, Jr.

TO: Gwendolyn Keyes Fleming
Regional Administrator, Region 4
U.S. Environmental Protection Agency

This is our report on the examination conducted by the Office of Inspector General of the
U.S. Environmental Protection Agency (EPA). We selected the North Carolina Rural Economic
Development Center, Inc., (NCREDC) for review. The purpose of the review was to determine
whether the NCREDC complied with grant requirements and applicable regulations. The Agency
provided a grant award to the NCREDC totaling $1,192,500. The report contains findings that
describe the problems the OIG has identified and corrective actions the OIG recommends. This
report represents the opinion of the OIG and does not necessarily represent the final EPA
position. EPA managers in accordance with established audit resolution procedures will make
final determination on matters in this report.

Action Required

In accordance with EPA Manual 2750, you are required to provide a written response to this
report within 120 calendar days, or by September 20, 2012. You should include a corrective
action plan for agreed-upon actions, including milestone dates. Your response will be posted on
the Office of Inspector General's public website, along with our memorandum commenting on
your response.

If you or your staff have any questions regarding this report, please contact Robert Adachi,
Director of Forensic Audits, at (415) 947-4537 or adachi.robert@epa.gov; or John Trefry,
Associate Director of Forensic Audits, at (202) 566-2474 or trefry.john@epa.gov.

Table of Contents

Appendices

Purpose

The purpose of this examination was to determine whether the costs claimed by the North Carolina Rural Economic Development Center, Inc. (NCREDC), under U.S. Environmental Protection Agency (EPA) Grant No. X96418405 were reasonable, allocable, and allowable; and whether the NCREDC's accounting and billing practices complied with the Code of Federal Regulations (CFR), specifically 2 CFR Part 230 (formerly Office of Management and Budget (OMB) Circular A-122, Cost Principles for Non-Profit Organizations).

Background

The mission of the NCREDC is to develop, promote, and implement sound economic strategies to improve the quality of life of rural North Carolinians. It serves the state's 85 rural counties, with a focus on individuals with low to moderate incomes and communities with limited resources. The NCREDC is a private, nonprofit organization funded by both public and private sources.

The NCREDC sought federal funding to partially support its *Water 2030 Initiative*, which had an estimated cost of $2,283,849. This initiative involved:

- Creating a state water budget, with projections for 2005 through 2030
- Analyzing updates
- Expanding water and sewer databases to include storm water and flood hazard data
- Funding for strategic education and communications support services

Ultimately, the NCREDC received funding from four sources for the project—EPA and three different State of North Carolina sources. Total project costs incurred for the *Water 2030 Initiative* were $2,204,031.

The fiscal year (FY) 2004 appropriations for EPA identified that the NCREDC would receive an earmark in the amount of $1,000,000. EPA Region 4 officials advised us that the initial grant award was reduced to $994,100. EPA's FY 2005 appropriation identified that the NCREDC would receive an additional earmark in the amount of $200,000. Region 4 advised us that this amount was reduced to $198,400, which made the total grant award $1,192,500.

On September 9, 2009, we issued a discussion draft report to the NCREDC and Region 4. The discussion draft report stated that the NCREDC did not comply with 2 CFR Part 230 with respect to financial management. In particular, the NCREDC:

- Did not properly allocate direct costs between state and federal funding sources
- Submitted requests for reimbursement that were not supported by its accounting records
- Claimed indirect costs without an approved indirect cost rate

The discussion draft concluded that EPA should recover all costs incurred ($1,192,500) under the grant. Both the NCREDC and Region 4 disagreed with the discussion draft findings. In its September 11, 2009, response, the NCREDC stated that the findings resulted from a misunderstanding about the manner in which costs were allocated to multiple funding sources, and from differences in its interpretations of regulations regarding federal grant administration. The NCREDC believes it spent EPA funds in an appropriate manner on a project of significance for the people of North Carolina.

At the time of the initial grant award, Region 4 was notified of the various funding sources and the estimated total costs of the *Water 2030 Initiative*. Region 4 recognized that the original grant application described the project as "North Carolina Water 2030" and that Grant No. X96418405 should have been awarded to include all funds associated with the complete project, including state funding sources. The region believes that the grant should have been awarded to include all funds associated with the complete project, reflecting the entire cost of $2,204,031, of which EPA was to pay $1,192,500.

In addition, Region 4 asserted that the $178,556 of questioned indirect costs would be eligible direct costs if the grantee executed a budget revision to remove the indirect costs and claim additional subcontract costs.

According to Region 4, the EPA project officer and EPA grants specialist contacted the grantee to reopen and revise the grant to address the concerns identified in the discussion draft report. On December 3, 2009, Region 4 reopened the grant and amended it to reflect full project cost of $2,204,031, minus indirect costs, and extended the budget/project period from December 31, 2007, to December 31, 2010.

On September 14, 2011, we issued a draft report to the NCREDC and Region 4. The draft report stated that the NCREDC did not comply with 2 CFR Part 230 with respect to financial management. Specifically, the NCREDC did not properly allocate direct costs between state and federal funding sources. The draft report concluded that EPA should recover all costs incurred ($1,192,500) under the grant. Both the NCREDC and Region 4 disagreed with the draft report findings.

We received responses to our draft report from the NCREDC and Region 4. Each commenter disagreed with our audit findings and corresponding recommendations, and in some cases, disagreed with each other. However, neither party provided any information that would cause the OIG to change its audit findings and recommendations.

Independent Attestation Report

As part of our continued oversight of grants awarded to nonprofit organizations by EPA, we examined the NCREDC's compliance with the requirements of 40 CFR Part 30, 2 CFR Part 230, and the terms and conditions applicable to the outlays reported in the Financial Status Report for Grant No. X96418405. The Financial Status Report covers the period October 1, 2003, to May 31, 2007. By signing the award documents, the grantee has accepted responsibility for complying with these requirements, and by signing the Financial Status Report the grantee certifies "... all outlays and unliquidated obligations are for the purposes set forth in the award documents." Our responsibility is to express an opinion on the grantee's compliance based on our examination.

Our examination was conducted in accordance with generally accepted government auditing standards issued by the Comptroller General of the United States. Our review was also conducted in accordance with attestation standards established by the American Institute of Certified Public Accountants and, accordingly, included examining, on a test basis, evidence supporting management's assertion and performing such other procedures as we deemed necessary in the circumstances. We believe that our examination provides a reasonable basis for our opinion. Field work was completed from March 9, 2009, through September 14, 2011.

We made site visits to EPA's Region 4 Office in Atlanta, Georgia, and performed the following steps:

- Reviewed EPA Grant No. X96418405, awarded to the NCREDC, and its modifications to determine criteria relevant to the examination
- Reviewed all payments made under the grant to determine whether there was a history of suspended or disallowed costs
- Reviewed files maintained by and conducted interviews with EPA's project officer and grants specialist to gather information concerning the NCREDC's performance under the subject grant

We made a site visit to the NCREDC office in Raleigh, North Carolina, and performed the following steps:

- Reviewed grantee support for the cumulative amounts reported for the period ended June 30, 2007, including the grantee's electronic accounting records, invoices, cancelled checks, and contracts
- Reviewed the grantee's supporting documentation for payment requests
- Conducted interviews of grantee personnel

We performed additional field work after the issuance of the discussion draft report, which involved the following steps:

- Reviewed the grantee's November 3, 2009, budget revision and justification documents
- Reviewed Region 4's December 3, 2009, Assistance Amendment and reviewed grant transactions through December 31, 2010
- Reviewed correspondence between the grantee and Region 4 personnel

As part of obtaining reasonable assurance that the recipient's costs claimed under the grant are free of material misstatement, we examined the NCREDC's compliance with the requirements of 40 CFR Part 30, 2 CFR Part 230, and the terms and conditions of the grant. We also considered the recipient's internal controls over cost reporting to determine our examination procedures and to express our opinion on the costs claimed. Our consideration of internal control would not necessarily disclose all internal control matters that might be a significant deficiency. A significant deficiency is a deficiency in internal control, or combination of control deficiencies, that adversely affects the recipient's ability to initiate, authorize, record, process, or report data reliably, in accordance with the applicable criteria or framework, such that there is more than a remote likelihood that a misstatement of the subject matter that is more than inconsequential will not be prevented or detected.

Our examination disclosed a significant deficiency concerning the recipient's internal controls and compliance with the requirements of 40 CFR Part 30 or 2 CFR Part 230. Our examination disclosed the NCREDC did not comply with 2 CFR Part 230 for financial management. Specifically, the NCREDC did not properly allocate direct costs between state and federal funding sources. As a result, we question costs of $1,192,500.

Robert K. Adachi

Robert K. Adachi
Director for Forensic Audits
May 23, 2012

Results of Examination

The NCREDC did not comply with 2 CFR Part 230 with respect to financial management. Specifically, the NCREDC did not properly allocate direct costs between state and federal funding sources. As a result, EPA should recover $1,192,500 in costs questioned under the grant. The NCREDC failed to properly allocate the questioned costs primarily because EPA provided incorrect guidance and inadequately monitored the grant. Additionally, the NCREDC was unfamiliar with federal grant regulations.

Initial Subcontract and Indirect Costs Claimed

In October 2007, the NCREDC submitted its initial final Financial Status Report identifying total outlays of $2,204,031 for the *Water 2030 Initiative*. Only a portion of the subcontract costs and all of the indirect costs were identified to the EPA grant. No indirect costs were charged to the other funding sources. There was no cost overrun associated with the *Water 2030 Initiative*. The Financial Status Report amounts were verified to the grantee's books and records (table 1).

Table 1: Costs claimed per grantee books and records

Cost element	Other funds	EPA funds	Total
Subcontract costs	$840,780	$1,013,944	$1,854,724
Other costs	170,751	0	170,751
Indirect costs	0	178,556	178,556
Total	$1,011,531	$1,192,500	$2,204,031

Source: NCREDC project cost records.

The NCREDC procured three subcontractors to perform work associated with the *Water 2030 Initiative*. Neither the subcontract agreements nor the vendor invoices specified whether activities were funded by EPA or the various state funding sources. The grantee did not have a methodology to allocate subcontract costs between EPA and state sources. When the NCREDC received an invoice, it allocated the entire invoice to one of its state sources and then arbitrarily assigned costs to the EPA grant. This process continued until all funds under the EPA grant were extinguished.

Without a methodology to allocate its subcontract costs between EPA and state sources, we could not determine, nor could the grantee demonstrate, that the costs charged to the EPA grant were allowable or allocable. Title 2 CFR Part 230, (formerly OMB Circular A-122, Cost Principles for Non-Profit Organizations), Appendix A, Section A4, states that a cost is allocable to a grant in accordance with the relative benefits received. Further, a cost is considered allocable to a federal award if the cost is treated consistently with other costs incurred for the same purpose in like circumstances. We concluded that the arbitrary cost allocations to the EPA grant were unsupported, unallowable, and not allocable. As a result, we questioned subcontract costs totaling $1,013,944.

Additionally, the NCREDC did not comply with the requirements of 2 CFR Part 230, Appendix A Section E, "Negotiation and Approval of Indirect Costs Rates," when developing its indirect cost rates. These regulations require nonprofits that have a previously established indirect cost rate to submit a new indirect cost proposal to their cognizant agency within 6 months after the close of each fiscal year. Because the NCREDC did not submit an indirect cost rate proposal as required, we questioned indirect costs of $178,556.

Budget Revision

The NCREDC disagreed with our initial discussion draft report. The NCREDC believed its cost allocations were supported and that the Agency reimbursed it for indirect costs throughout the grant term without question. The NCREDC assumed that EPA had approved the requested indirect rates.

Region 4 believed that the amounts appropriated by Congress in FYs 2004 and 2005 to the NCREDC totaled a fixed amount of $1,192,500, which was the exact amount EPA paid the NCREDC at the initial grant close-out. The region believed that:

- The work the NCREDC completed was consistent with the appropriation language, grant application, and grant award documents
- The grantee incurred subcontract costs beyond the amount allowed in the grant
- The questioned indirect costs could be removed from the claim and be replaced by allowable subcontract costs if the grantee requested a budget revision

Region 4 officials requested that the grantee submit a revised budget. On November 3, 2009, the NCREDC submitted a revised budget and justification documents. Based on this information, the region reopened the grant and issued an amendment on December 3, 2009. The explanation of changes stated, "The grant is modified to show total eligible project costs and exclude indirect costs as a result of an audit resolution." The revised budget is summarized in table 2:

Table 2: *Water 2030 Initiative* 2009 budget revision

Cost element	Other funds	EPA funds	Total
Subcontract costs	$716,916	$1,192,500	$1,909,416
Other costs	116,059	0	116,059
Indirect costs	0	0	0
Total	$832,975	$1,192,500	$2,025,475

Source: NCREDC Revised Grant Budget, 2009.

We noted the following differences between the grantee books and records (table 1) and the revised budget (table 2):

- The revised budget removed indirect costs and reduced total outlays by $178,556
- The revised budget increased EPA funded subcontracts by $178,556.
- The revised budget reduced total costs funded by other sources by $178,556

The NCREDC stated that the expenses reflected in the original grant close-out, which included subcontract costs identified to EPA of $1,013,944, reflected the proper and planned allocation of costs on a consistent basis between the various federal and state funding sources in accordance with the overall project budget and the budget in the grant agreement. However, based on Region 4's direction, the NCREDC submitted a revised budget that does not agree with its books and records, and does not reflect the proper and planned allocation of costs between the various federal and state funding sources. Clearly, the revised budget shifted costs that were identified to state funding sources to the EPA grant.

The NCREDC revised budget shifted $178,556 of subcontract costs allocable to state funding sources to the EPA grant. Title 2 CFR Part 230, Appendix A, Section A4, states that a cost is allocable to a grant in accordance with the relative benefits received. We determined that the additional subcontract costs allocated to the EPA grant were unsupported, unallowable, and not allocable. As a result, we question additional subcontract costs totaling $178,556.

Neither Region 4 nor the NCREDC provided an explanation for this cost shift. The Agency approved the revision without question. We believe the improper cost shifting was caused by Region 4's improper guidance and the NCREDC's unfamiliarity with federal grant regulations.

Recommendation

We recommend that the Regional Administrator, EPA Region 4:

1. Disallow all costs associated with Grant No. X96418405 and recover $1,192,500 of costs paid to the NCREDC.

Region 4 and NCREDC Responses

The Office of Inspector General (OIG) received comments to the draft report from Region 4 and the NCREDC.

Region 4 disagreed with the findings in the draft report. Specifically, the region:

- Believes that the questioned costs are allowable because the initial grant was to fund the subcontractors associated with the gathering of data and its evaluation of the project
- Does not agree with disallowing all funding because the recipient was able to provide source documentation for the expended costs, which are eligible
- Asserts that it reviewed all subcontractor invoices of expenditures and determined that the costs were correct, reasonable, and allowable in accordance with OMB Cost Principles and 2 CFR Part 230.

Additionally, the region proposes an alternative action plan to address the disallowance of costs. In this plan, the NCREDC would be required to submit a corrective action plan to include the methodology for full accounting of the allocation of costs among state and federal funding sources for the full project costs, thereby determining the reasonableness, allocability, and allowability of costs in accordance with the provisions of the applicable federal cost principles. The full text of Region 4's comments and the OIG's responses are included in appendix A.

The NCREDC also disagreed with the findings in the draft report. Specifically, the NCREDC asserts that:

- The costs incurred under this grant were not allocated arbitrarily; they were allocated among federal and state funding sources in accordance with the budget originally submitted to EPA
- It submitted indirect cost rate proposals to the Agency with its grant applications and believes that if the Agency should have prepared a formal written agreement regarding the NCREDC's indirect cost rates the OIG should take this up with the Agency.

The full text of the NCREDC's comments and the OIG's responses are included in appendix B.

OIG Comment on Region 4 and NCREDC Responses

We evaluated the information in the responses to the draft report. Based on this evaluation, we did not modify our report findings or our recommendation. Therefore, the recommendation is unresolved with resolution efforts in progress.

The region provided a corrective action plan in which the NCREDC will submit a plan outlining full accounting of the allocation of costs between state and federal funding sources for the project so that the region can determine the reasonableness, allocability, and allowability of costs in accordance with the provisions of the applicable federal cost principles. Although we agree with the region's plan, the region must recognize that the $178,556 budget revision it directed is not allocable to the EPA grant because it shifted subcontract costs allocable to state funding sources to the EPA grant. Further, Region 4's plan must acknowledge that the original subcontract costs allocated to the grant were not allocated in accordance with the grantee's original allocation plan.

We added comments to the Region 4 and NCREDC responses, which are included as appendices, to illustrate our position.

Status of Recommendations and Potential Monetary Benefits

		RECOMMENDATIONS				POTENTIAL MONETARY BENEFITS (in $000s)	
Rec. No.	Page No.	Subject	Status[1]	Action Official	Planned Completion Date	Claimed Amount	Agreed To Amount
1	7	Disallow all costs associated with Grant No. X96418405 and recover $1,192,500 of costs paid to the NCREDC.	U	Regional Administrator, Region 4		$1,192	

[1] O = recommendation is open with agreed-to corrective actions pending
C = recommendation is closed with all agreed-to actions completed
U = recommendation is unresolved with resolution efforts in progress

Region 4 Response and OIG Evaluation

<u>**MEMORANDUM**</u>

SUBJECT: EPA Region 4 Response to Draft Audit Report:
Costs Claimed by the North Carolina Rural
Economic Development Center, Inc., Under
EPA Grant No. X96418405
Project No. OA-FY09-A-0873

FROM: Gwendolyn Keyes Fleming
Regional Administrator

TO: Robert Adachi, Director of Forensic Audits
EPA - Office of Inspector General

The purpose of this memorandum is to respond to the September 14, 2011, draft report issued by the Office of Inspector General recommending that the Environmental Protection Agency disallow all costs paid under the earmark Environmental Program Management Grant No. X96418405 to the North Carolina Rural Economic Development Center, Inc. (NCREDC) and recover $1,192,500. We reviewed the report issued by your office and compared your findings to the information available in the project file and supplemental information provided by the grantee. Based on this information, we offer the following response to your draft findings:

1. Pursuant to 40 CFR 30.23, the EPA shall not require cost sharing or matching unless required by statute, regulation, Executive Order or official agency policy. This grant was awarded under Section 104(b) of the Clean Water Act which does not require matching funds. The match provided by the State, the Clean Water Management Trust Fund and the NCREDC was voluntary. Therefore, the original award and subsequent funding actions, prior to the audit finding, only reflected the federal funding indicated in the recipient's application (SF-424) with a voluntary five percent match. As stated in the administrative conditions of the May 25, 2006, amendment, "This award and the resulting ratio of funding is based on estimated costs requested in the application. The EPA participation in the final total allowable program/project costs (outlays) shall not exceed the statutory limitation (100) percent of total allowable program/project costs or the total funds awarded, whichever is lower."

> **OIG Response:** The OIG agrees that the grantee was awarded the appropriated amount of the grant and that there is no matching funds requirement under Section 104(b) of the Clean Water Act. We note the disagreement between the region and the NCREDC as to whether the matching fund requirement was voluntary (region's position) or required (NCREDC's position). We believe the region and the NCREDC should resolve this issue during audit resolution.

2. We believe the costs are allowable, because the initial grant was to fund the contractors associated with the gathering of data and its evaluation for the project as described in the appropriations language and grant application and workplan. In completing the grant, the recipient accomplished the environmental outputs and outcomes delineated in the original workplan; thus, providing the EPA with the anticipated deliverables.

OIG Response: The OIG agrees that the NCREDC accomplished the intent of the grant. We disagree that the grant funds were solely identified to NCREDC contact costs. Grant documents clearly identify that Region 4 provided funding for approximately 61 percent of the contractor costs and 100 percent of the indirect costs estimated by the NCREDC.

3. We do not concur with disallowing all the EPA's funding, in the amount of $1,192,500, because the recipient was able to provide source documentation for the expended cost, which is an eligible cost. Further, we feel the disallowance of cost simply based on the methodology for allocation, does not warrant the disallowance of all total cost.

OIG Response: The OIG agrees that the NCREDC provided source documentation for its incurred subcontract costs. However, we do not agree that the subcontract costs incurred were eligible costs. Neither the subcontract agreements nor the vendor invoices specified whether activities were funded by EPA or the various state funding sources. The grantee's proposed methodology to allocate subcontract costs between EPA and state funding sources was not used. When the NCREDC received an invoice, it allocated the entire invoice to one of its state sources and then arbitrarily assigned costs to the EPA grant. This process continued until all funds under the EPA grant were extinguished.

Without following its proposed methodology to allocate subcontract costs between EPA and state sources, we could not determine, nor could the NCREDC demonstrate, that the costs charged to the EPA grant were allowable or allocable. Title 2 CFR Part 230 (formerly OMB Circular A-122, Cost Principles for Non-Profit Organizations), Appendix A, Section A4, states that a cost is allocable to a grant in accordance with the relative benefits received. Further, a cost is considered allocable to a federal award if the cost is treated consistently with other costs incurred for the same purpose in like circumstances. We concluded that the arbitrary cost allocations to the EPA grant were unsupported, unallowable, and not allocable. As a result, we questioned subcontract costs totaling $1,013,944.

Additionally, the OIG disagrees that the NCREDC indirect costs are eligible costs. The NCREDC did not comply with the requirements of 2 CFR Part 230, Appendix A Section E, "Negotiation and Approval of Indirect Costs Rates," when developing its indirect cost rates. These regulations require nonprofits that have a previously established indirect cost rate to submit a new indirect cost proposal to their cognizant agency within 6 months after the close of each fiscal year. Because the NCREDC did not submit its indirect cost rates in the form of a request for approval, nor did the Agency take any actions to approve the rates, we questioned indirect costs of $178,556.

4. The review of the single audit report was conducted during Region 4's pre-award and post award phase. The organization's established practices and financial management system met the requirements as indicated in the financial reviews of the independent auditor, as required in accordance with Office of Management and Budget (OMB) Circular A133, Single Audit Act. Please note, the reports did not reveal any material weaknesses or findings.

OIG Response: The OIG agrees that the single audit reports did not reveal any material weaknesses or findings; however, a single audit is not designed to detect all material weaknesses that might exist. The purpose of a single audit is to express an opinion on the "financial statements and not to provide assurance on internal controls over financial reporting." The single audit states that its consideration of the internal control over financial reporting would not necessarily disclose all matters in the internal control that might be material weaknesses.

5. Based on our review of the submitted documentation, all contractor invoices of expenditures were documented (traceable) and correct and deemed reasonable and allowable in accordance with applicable OMB Cost Principles, 2 CFR 230 (formerly A-122).

OIG Response: Title 2 CFR Part 230, Appendix A Section A, "Basic Considerations," requires a cost to be both reasonable and allocable—a requirement not included in the regional review. As documented above, neither the subcontract costs nor the indirect costs claimed by the NCREDC are allocable to the EPA grant. Without following its proposed methodology to allocate subcontract costs between EPA and state funding sources, the NCREDC could not demonstrate that the costs charged to the EPA grant were allowable or allocable. Further, because the NCREDC never requested approval of its indirect rates, and no written rate agreement exists, the claimed indirect costs are unallowable.

Corrective Actions:
1. As a result of an October 5, 2009, conference call with John Trefry, and in an email to John Trefry and Philip Cleveland on October 26, 2009, Region 4 agreed to reopen the grant and amend it to reflect the full project cost minus indirect costs, of which the EPA's share was $1,192,500. Additionally, the recipient submitted a revised budget eliminating the cost allocated for indirect charges by reallocating the cost in other budget categories (direct) and provided supporting documentation and invoices. The grant was amended on December 1, 2009.

OIG Response: Although informed of the region's intent to reopen the grant, the OIG did not concur or nonconcur with the region's actions. EPA Manual 2750, Chapter 3, "Resolution of OIG Reports of Assistance Agreement," Paragraph 6f, "Instances When OIG Concurrence Is Required Before the Action Official Issues the Management Decision," states, "All OIG reports in which the aggregate value of Questioned Costs exceeds or is equal to $250,000 require OIG concurrence on the proposed Management Decision before the Action Official issues it to the assistance recipient." There was no OIG concurrence with the Agency's plan. Had the region requested concurrence on the proposed Management Decision before taking action with NCREDC, the proposed action would have been denied.

2. As a result of the initial audit report in September 2009, Region 4 designated the recipient, NCREDC, as a "high risk" grantee in accordance with 40 CFR 30.14 and will impose a special grant condition on all future awards.

> **OIG Response:** The OIG concurs with this action.

3. As an alternative action to the disallowance of cost in the amount of $1,192,500, we recommend the recipient submit a corrective action plan to include the methodology full accounting of the allocation of costs among state and federal funding sources for the full project cost; thereby, determining the reasonableness, allocability and allowability of costs in accordance with the provisions of the applicable Federal cost principles.

> **OIG Response:** The proposed action suggests that the region does not believe that the NCREDC has fully accounted for the costs incurred or their subsequent allocation to the grant. However, in its previous statements above, the region has argued the opposite; namely, that all costs were allowable and allocable.
>
> The region provided a corrective action plan in which the NCREDC will submit a plan outlining full accounting of the allocation of costs between state and federal funding sources for the project, so that the region can determine the reasonableness, allocability and allowability of costs in accordance with the provisions of the applicable federal cost principles. Although we agree with the region's plan, the region must recognize that the $178,556 budget revision it directed is not allocable to the EPA grant because it shifted subcontract costs allocable to state funding sources to the EPA grant. Further, Region 4's plan must acknowledge that the original subcontract costs allocated to the grant were not allocated in accordance with the grantee's original allocation plan.

Recommendation:

We recommend that the costs associated with grant X96418405 continue to be allowed. If you have any further questions regarding this response, please contact James D. Giattina at 404-562-9345.

> **OIG Response:** The OIG does not concur and continues to question all costs associated with the grant in its entirety. The region's response failed to demonstrate that the subcontractor costs charged to the EPA grant were allowable or allocable. Further, the region's response did not address the allowability of any indirect cost.

cc: Arthur A. Elkins, Jr., OIG
       Mike Hill, OIG

NCREDC Response and OIG Evaluation

North Carolina Rural Economic Development Center, Inc.
Response to Draft Report

Costs Claimed by the North Carolina Rural Economic Development Center, Inc.
Under EPA Grant X96418405

Project No. OA-FY09-A-0873
September 14, 2011

Subcontract Costs Claimed

In its draft report issued September 14, 2011, the EPA OIG asserts that "The NCREDC did not comply with Title 2 CFR Part 230 for financial management. Specifically, the NCREDC did not properly allocate direct costs between state and federal funding sources." Furthermore, the report asserts that "when NCREDC received an invoice, it allocated the entire invoice to one of its state sources and then arbitrarily assigned costs to the EPA grant. This process continued until all funds under the EPA grant were extinguished."

We disagree with these statements. The costs incurred under this grant were not allocated arbitrarily; they were allocated among the Federal and State funding sources in accordance with the budget originally submitted to EPA.

The basis for the allocation of costs was a comprehensive budget for the Water 2030 project that was developed at the conception of this initiative, as partners for this project were being identified. This budget included anticipated funding from EPA, the North Carolina Clean Water Management Trust Fund and funds appropriated to NCREDC from the North Carolina General Assembly. Included with this response is a copy of the detailed project budget (Exhibit 1) as it was revised through September 21, 2004, which was the basis for preparation of the initial application for EPA earmark funding submitted on September 27, 2004.

At the time the initial application for funding was prepared and submitted, NCREDC was instructed by the Atlanta Region 4 office of EPA to include in the application budget only the amount of EPA funding plus enough additional cost to satisfy the 5% matching requirement. Therefore the application budget included only $1,046,421 in total costs divided between the contractual and indirect cost line items.

> **OIG Response:** As noted in the comments to Region 4's response, the region and the NCREDC disagree as to whether the matching fund requirement was voluntary (region's position) or required (NCREDC's position). We believe the region and the NCREDC should resolve this issue during audit resolution.

Following submission of the application but prior to grant issuance, NCREDC received a request from Shirley Grayer in the Atlanta Region 4 office for an overall project budget. A condensed form of the overall project budget was submitted by NCREDC to Ms. Grayer on December 4, 2004. A copy of this condensed budget is included in this report (Exhibit 2). The condensed budget contained the same information as Exhibit 1 but simply combined the column titled "Needed Additional Funds" from the detailed project budget with the "Matching Funds – Rural Center" column. The amount of the "Needed Additional Funds" column in the detailed budget was the basis for requesting the second earmark.

Although the condensed budget was supplied to the Atlanta Region 4 office, EPA's initial grant document issued on December 21, 2004 included only the federal portion of the overall budget and the required 5% match. It consisted of only two line items – contractual services and indirect costs. Even though the grant document did not include the funding details, information previously provided by NCREDC to EPA clearly indicates the planned methodology for allocation of overall project costs among all funding sources available for this project.

> **OIG Response:** Based on the data provided in its response, we agree that the grantee provided sufficient information to Region 4 to detail its planned project budget and the various funding sources associated with the *Water 2030 Initiative*. We further recognize that the intent of the EPA grant was to pay for approximately 61 percent of the work of the consulting engineers (subcontractors) plus applicable indirect costs. The grantee's planned methodology shows that a portion of the subcontract costs are not allocable to the EPA grant.

Exhibit 3 summarizes the invoices paid to each subcontractor for each reporting period, and the allocation of those invoices among the Federal and State funding sources. The accounting records demonstrate that posted expenditures were routinely analyzed and appropriate adjustments were made at each quarter end prior to submission of reimbursement requests. This quarterly analysis and adjustment was performed using the overall project budget (Exhibit 1) as guidance for an appropriate allocation. The attached reports from the NCREDC accounting system (Exhibit 4) demonstrate that the reimbursement requests submitted agree with the underlying accounting records.

It is true that for administrative convenience, every invoice was not divided pro rata among the various funding sources. Rather, during the course of the project, each invoice received and paid was allocated to a single funding source in accordance with the project budget. The initial pay request under this grant was submitted on January 28, 2005 for the reporting period ending December 31, 2004. At that date, all subcontractor costs budgeted for payment by the Clean Water Management Trust Fund to Hobbs and McGill had been expended and charged to that funding source, and the remaining balance of payments made to those two subcontractors had been charged to EPA. By the time the second request for payment was made in April 2005, all of the state funds budgeted for payment to AMEC under the initial earmark grant had been expended. Once the budgeted funds from CWMTF and the State had been exhausted, all subsequent subcontractor invoices were allocated to EPA up to the remaining balance of funds available under the initial earmark grant. The end result was that the charges by these subcontractors were properly allocated between the EPA and state grants as shown on the original budget.

OIG Response: Based on the information provided in its response, we do not agree that the costs were allocated in accordance with the original plan.

The budget for this project identified the following cost allocations for each subcontractor:

Subcontractor	Total amount budgeted	EPA share	Percentage	Other share	Percentage
No. 1	$ 870,000	$ 638,944	73%	$ 231,056	27%
No. 2	400,000	187,500	47%	212,500	53%
No. 3	400,000	187,500	47%	212,500	53%
Totals	$ 1,670,000	$ 1,013,944		$ 656,056	

The actual costs incurred per the grantee's records showed the following allocations:

Subcontractor	Total amount incurred	EPA share	Percentage	Other share	Percentage
No. 1	$ 980,326	$ 693,944	71%	$ 286,382	29%
No. 2	400,000	147,500	37%	252,500	63%
No. 3	400,000	172,500	43%	227,500	57%
Totals	$ 1,780,326	$ 1,013,944		$ 766,382	

As shown above, the total subcontract costs were greater than the budgeted amounts. Although the total allocation of subcontract costs to the Agency agrees with the budgeted amounts, the individual allocations by subcontractor differ, indicating that the NCREDC did not follow its initial allocation plan.

Per its response, NCREDC asserts that for administrative convenience, every invoice was not divided pro rata among the various funding sources. Rather, during the course of the project, each invoice received and paid was allocated to a single funding source in accordance with the project budget. The end result was that the charges by these subcontractors were properly allocated between the EPA and state grants as shown on the original budget. The above analysis clearly shows that the NCREDC did not allocate costs as shown on the original budget.

In September 2005, NCREDC applied for additional EPA grant funds available under the second earmark. These funds were added to the original grant in an amendment that was issued in May 2006. The amended grant budget issued by EPA again excluded all funding sources other than EPA and contained only two line items – contractual services and indirect costs. During the final project reporting quarter ending June 30, 2006, remaining subcontractor expenses were allocated between state sources and EPA in accordance with the overall project budget.

We firmly believe that NCREDC did not "arbitrarily assign costs to funding sources" and did in fact have a reasonable, documented and supportable methodology for allocation of subcontract costs between federal and state funding sources. The basis for allocation of these costs was the overall project budget, which was available in EPA's file.

> **OIG Response:** We agree that the NCREDC had a methodology for the allocation of subcontract costs; however, we determined that the methodology was not used. When the NCREDC received an invoice, it allocated the entire invoice to one of its state sources and then arbitrarily assigned costs to the EPA grant. This process continued until all funds under the EPA grant were extinguished.
>
> Without following its proposed methodology to allocate subcontract costs between EPA and state sources, we could not determine, nor could the NCREDC demonstrate, that the costs charged to the EPA grant were allowable or allocable.

Indirect Costs

At the time NCREDC applied for and received this EPA grant, no "cognizant agency" had been appointed for the purpose of setting an indirect cost rate to be used by the center with all federal agencies. The federal funding NCREDC had historically received had been single year, project-based grants that varied significantly from year to year in amount and with regard to the funding agency. We had been unsuccessful in our attempts to have a funding agency formally negotiate a rate with us. Historically, indirect cost rates for Federal grants received had been approved by the funding agency based on submission of a cost allocation plan without execution of a formal negotiation agreement.

> **OIG Response:** The OIG concurs with the first part this statement. We do not know how indirect costs were approved in the past by other funding agencies.

Title 2 CFR Part 230, Appendix A, Section E, subparagraph E.2.b. requires that "A non-profit which has not previously established an indirect cost rate with a Federal agency shall submit its initial indirect cost proposal immediately after the organization is advised that an award will be made and, in no event, later than three months after the effective date of the award." NCREDC met this requirement. It included a copy of its indirect cost rate proposal, based on the center's June 30, 2001 financial statements, with the original grant application for funding submitted in September 2004. Furthermore, in September 2005 when NCREDC submitted an application to EPA for funding from the second earmark, it included with that application a new indirect cost rate proposal based on the center's June 30, 2004 financial statements. When EPA made the initial and amended grant awards, it accepted the center's proposal by reflecting the proposed indirect costs in Table A of the grant award document, in the column entitled "Total Approved Allowable Budget Period Cost." Throughout the term of the grant, EPA reimbursed NCREDC for the indirect costs claimed without question. If OIG concludes that EPA should have prepared a formal written agreement regarding the center's indirect cost rates, it should direct it's concerns to EPA.

> **OIG Response:** The NCREDC submitted its FY 2001 Cost Allocation Plan/Indirect Cost Rate Proposal, dated February 21, 2002, to the Agency on December 2, 2004, prior to the grant award. Title 2 CFR Part 230, Appendix A, Section E, Subparagraph 1.f, defines an indirect cost proposal as the documentation prepared by an organization to substantiate its claim for the reimbursement of indirect costs. This proposal provides the basis for the review and negotiation leading to the establishment of an organization's indirect cost rate. Title 2 CFR Part 230, Appendix A, Section E, Subparagraph 2.g, requires indirect rate negotiations to be formalized in a written agreement between the cognizant agency and the non-profit organization.
>
> The NCREDC's submission did not request that the Agency review or approve the submitted rate, and no written rate agreement between the EPA and the NCREDC exists. The NCREDC's FY 2001 Cost Allocation Plan/Indirect Cost Rate Proposal appears to support the indirect rate proposed in its grant application.
>
> The NCREDC external auditors prepared a 2004 Cost Allocation Plan/Indirect Cost Rate Proposal on February 9, 2005. The NCREDC did not request that the Agency review or approve this rate, and no written rate agreement between EPA and the NCREDC exits. The NCREDC only submitted this updated plan to the Agency when it submitted an application for additional funding.

We did not submit follow-up indirect cost rate calculations during successive years of the grant because we did not have an indirect cost rate that had been formally established with a cognizant agency. Subparagraph E.2.c. states that "Organizations that *have previously established indirect cost rates* must submit a new indirect cost proposal to the cognizant agency within six months after the close of the fiscal year." Since we did not have a formally established rate with a cognizant agency, no such submission was required.

> **OIG Response:** Title 2 CFR Part 230, Appendix A, Section E, Negotiation and Approval of Indirect Cost rates, requires a non-profit organization that has not previously established an indirect cost rate with a federal agency to submit its initial indirect cost proposal immediately after the organization is advised that an award will be made. Further, organizations that have previously established indirect cost rates must submit a new indirect cost proposal to the cognizant agency within 6 months after the close of each fiscal year. Because the NCREDC did not submit its indirect cost rates in the form of a request for approval, nor did the Agency take any actions to approve the proposed rates, we questioned indirect costs of $178,556.

Budget Revision

NCREDC received OIG's original Discussion Draft report for review of grant #96418405 on September 9, 2009. We disagreed with the findings in the report and responded formally on September 11, 2009. We discussed our response with the OIG auditors on September 15, 2009. Following that discussion, NCREDC believed that all issues would be resolved favorably, except for the indirect cost claim.

On September 17, 2009 we received a call from the OIG auditor to say that they were discussing the matter with the Atlanta Region 4 office of EPA. On September 29, 2009 we received a call from Artie Buff with the Atlanta Region 4 office asking us to submit a revised application with a budget showing all grant costs paid by EPA as contractual service costs, eliminating the claim for reimbursement of indirect costs. We submitted the revised application on October 14, 2009 and executed an amendment to the grant agreement on December 4, 2009. We also submitted a revised final pay request to correspond with the amended grant agreement. We had understood from earlier conversations with the OIG auditors that this would resolve the indirect cost issue.

OIG Response: On October 5, 2009, Region 4 officials advised the OIG that the region was reviewing its options to address the draft report, including reopening the grant and moving all indirect costs claimed to the direct category. In accordance with EPA Manual 2750, the region was requested to provide the OIG a written response to the September 2009 discussion draft report findings and recommendations. The OIG did not receive a response from the region. Any agreements reached between Region 4 and the NCREDC regarding this matter are outside established Agency procedures and have not been agreed to by the OIG.

Had the region requested concurrence on the proposed Management Decision before taking action with NCREDC, the proposed action would have been denied. The NCREDC revised budget does not agree with its books and records, and does not reflect the planned allocation of costs between the various federal and state funding sources. The revised budget shifted costs that were identified to state funding sources to the EPA grant. Although the proposed action would have eliminated the questioned indirect costs, it would have replaced those costs with additional subcontract costs that were unsupported, unallowable, and not allocable to the EPA grant. (See "Budget Revision," pages 6–7 of this report.)

Shifting the indirect costs from the EPA grant to a State grant created no problems for the State funding sources. As OIG is aware, NCREDC sought funding for the Water 2030 project from EPA and the North Carolina Clean Water Management Trust Fund. Additional funding to complete the project was to come from recurring annual state appropriations for the years ended June 30, 2005 and June 30, 2006 of $100,000 each for water management projects, or from other previously appropriated funds designated for funding capacity grants and other capacity building measures. The state capacity funding was the final source of funding available to be used for the project. This appropriated funding was flexible and could also be used by NCREDC for other types of infrastructure grants and technical assistance activities.

OIG Response: According to NCREDC, indirect costs were not an allowable cost under state funding sources and its various indirect rate proposals do not include state programs in the overhead allocation base. Our review of the project cost records confirmed that no charges for indirect costs were made to state sources. "Shifting" indirect costs to a state grant would be noncompliant with NCREDC's originally submitted cost allocation plans.

As noted in the report, the revised budget shifted $178,556 of costs allocable to state funding sources to the EPA grant. The additional subcontract costs allocated to the EPA grant were unsupported, unallowable, and not allocable.

The NCREDC stated that the expenses reflected in its original grant close-out, which included subcontract costs identified to EPA of $1,013,944, reflected the proper and planned allocation of costs on a consistent basis between the various federal and state funding sources in accordance with the overall project budget and the budget in the grant agreement. However, based on Region 4's direction, the NCREDC submitted a revised budget that does not agree with its books and records, and does not reflect the proper and planned allocation of costs between the various federal and state funding sources. The revised budget shifted costs that were identified to state funding sources to the EPA grant.

Under specific instruction from Atlanta Region 4 staff, we eliminated indirect costs charged to the grant and substituted allowable and allocable direct costs. We charged an additional $178,556 of contractual services costs to EPA and reversed the indirect cost recovery income we had posted for the grant. In revising this report, NCREDC did report contract cost previously charged to the state capacity funding source to EPA. This was recorded in our financial statements at June 30, 2010 in consultation with our auditors as a reclassification between unrestricted and temporarily restricted net assets. The impact of this was to reduce our unrestricted net assets and to increase temporarily restricted net assets in the capacity grant funding category, making these funds available to support other infrastructure grants and technical assistance activities. We believed, based on the guidance given by the Atlanta Region 4 staff, that this action constituted an appropriate resolution to the indirect cost issue that had been agreed to by OIG.

Distribution

Regional Administrator, Region 4
Agency Follow-Up Official (the CFO)
Agency Follow-Up Coordinator
Director, Office of Financial Management, Office of the Chief Financial Officer
Director, Grants and Interagency Agreements Management Division, Office of Administration
     and Resources Management
Chief, Grants, Finance, and Cost Recovery Branch, Region 4
Audit Follow-Up Coordinator, Region 4
Director, Office of External Affairs, Region 4
President, NCREDC
Vice President, Finance and Administration, NCREDC

ARMY CIVIL AFFAIRS FUNCTIONAL SPECIALISTS: ON THE VERGE OF
EXTINCTION

The United States' post conflict efforts in Afghanistan and Iraq have generated

new initiatives to prepare the United States Government (USG) and the military,

particularly the Army, for stability operations. The effort to create USG capabilities to

conduct stability operations in a more unified and coherent fashion rests on the central

idea that, as part of the United States strategy to deal with transnational terrorist groups,

the U.S. must have the capabilities to assist governments or regions under serious

stress. Weak or failed states and ungoverned territories can create a threat to U.S.

national security or interests as we have seen with the terrorist attacks of September

11th and piracy off the coast of Somalia.[1] During stability operations, the primary focus

of U.S. policy carried out by U.S. military forces, civilian government agencies, and

multinational partners, will be on helping a severely stressed government avoid failure

or recover from a devastating natural disaster, or on assisting an emerging host nation

government in building new security, economic and political institutions and processes.

Department of Defense (DOD) policy establishes stability operations as a core

military mission and assigns it the same priority as combat operations to be integrated

across all DOD activities including doctrine, organizations, training, education,

exercises, material, leadership, personnel, facilities, and planning.[2] A key policy point is

that U.S. military forces shall be prepared to perform all tasks necessary to establish or

maintain order when civilians cannot do so. The DOD will have the capability to ensure

that when directed, it can establish civil security, civil control, restore or provide

essential services, repair critical infrastructure, and provide humanitarian assistance.[3]

To this end, the Army initiated a major shift in Army doctrine by establishing full spectrum operations as the central tenet of how it applies its capabilities. Stability and civil support operations are no longer something that the Army conducts "other than war." Army forces must address the civil situation directly and continuously by specialized activities and civil-military operations that are of equal importance to offense and defense operations.[4] Stability operations are military missions, tasks, and activities conducted outside the United States to maintain or reestablish a safe and secure environment and to provide essential governmental services, emergency infrastructure reconstruction, and humanitarian relief.[5] Additionally, the Army must plan for and be prepared to govern on an interim basis when conditions are not favorable for the introduction of civilian instruments of national power. U.S. interagency partners do not have the expeditionary capability to operate alongside military personnel in hostile environments and there is no plan to build this capacity.[6]

The Army capability that plays the most crucial role in stability operations is Civil Affairs (CA).[7] Years ago the primary role of CA was reducing foreign civilian interference with U.S. military operations. Now Civil Affairs accelerate stability by helping to restore and maintain public order; safeguarding, mobilizing and using local resources; facilitating the equitable distribution of humanitarian supplies and services, and other critical functions involving essential services and governance.[8] If the Army and DOD want to increase their capability to perform stability operations, then Civil Affairs is clearly a capability to focus on. When examining how well DOD and the Army have institutionalized the military capabilities to support stability operations, an increase in the number of Civil Affairs forces has been touted as one of the organizational efforts